HIP-HOP Biographies

PHARRELL

SADDLEBACK
EDUCATIONAL PUBLISHING

Beyoncé	Nicki Minaj
Chris Brown	**Pharrell**
Sean Combs	Pitbull
Drake	Rihanna
Dr. Dre	Usher
50 Cent	Lil Wayne
Jay Z	Kanye West

SADDLEBACK
EDUCATIONAL PUBLISHING
www.sdlback.com

ISBN-13: 978-1-62250-926-3
ISBN-10: 1-62250-926-9
eBook: 978-1-63078-048-7

Printed in Singapore by Craft Print International Ltd
0000/CA00000000
19 18 17 16 15 1 2 3 4 5

Table of Contents

Timeline

1973: Pharrell is born on April 5th in Virginia Beach, Virginia.

1985: Pharrell meets Chad Hugo. They form a lasting relationship and will go on to make music as N.E.R.D. and the Neptunes.

1998: Pharrell catches the attention of the music world when he produces Noreaga's song "Superthug."

2001: The Neptunes gain global success with Britney Spears's "I'm a Slave 4 U." N.E.R.D. releases their debut album *In Search Of...*

2002: The Neptunes win Producer of the Year at both the Source Awards and the Billboard Music Awards.

2004: N.E.R.D. releases *Fly or Die.*

2005: Together with Japanese artist Nigo, Pharrell debuts two clothing lines called Billionaire Boys Club and Icecream. Pharrell is voted the World's Best Dressed Man by *Esquire magazine*.

2006: Pharrell releases his first solo album, *In My Mind*.

2008: Rocket Ayer Williams, Pharrell's son, is born. Pharrell designs sunglasses and jewelry for Louis Vuitton.

2010: Pharrell and Hans Zimmer compose the music for the movie *Despicable Me*.

2011: Pharrell creates the documentary *Tokyo Rising* about the massive earthquake and tsunami that hit Japan earlier that year.

2012: Pharrell launches *i am OTHER*, a multimedia group. Pharrell publishes his book *Pharrell: Places and Spaces I've Been.*

2013: Pharrell marries his longtime girlfriend, Helen Lasichanh. He has record-setting hits with Robin Thicke's "Blurred Lines" and Daft Punk's "Get Lucky." Pharrell works on the soundtrack for *Despicable Me 2*. He releases the 24-hour music video "Happy." The video gets nearly 400 million views on YouTube.

2014: Pharrell releases his second solo album, *G I R L*. He wins seven awards, including a Grammy for Producer of the Year. Pharrell signs an exclusive contract with Adidas. The mayor of Virginia Beach presents Pharrell with the key to the city and names June 7, 2014, Pharrell Williams Day.

Seeing Sounds

Many people know Pharrell Williams as a rapper and fashion icon. Few people realize that Pharrell has changed the way popular music sounds with his innovative music production.

Pharrell was a creative and curious child. He loved hip-hop, but his life wasn't shaped by the streets. So he made hip-hop that fit his own experience. He followed his passion for music, for skateboarding, and for space exploration.

Pharrell Williams was born on April 5, 1973, in Virginia Beach, Virginia. His mother, Carolyn, was a teacher, and his father, Pharaoh, was a handyman. Pharrell's parents worked long hours and did not make a lot of money. Pharrell said that his family ate "a lot of pork and beans" to make the food budget stretch between paychecks.

Pharrell has two younger brothers named Cato and Psolomon. There are gaps of 10 years between each child. Later, his parents divorced and his father remarried. From his father's second marriage, Pharrell has two younger half-brothers, Pharoah and David.

As a child, Pharrell spent a lot of time on his own. The TV became his best friend. One of his favorite things to watch was the Jackson 5 video for "Shake Your Body (Down to the Ground)." Pharrell dreamed about music.

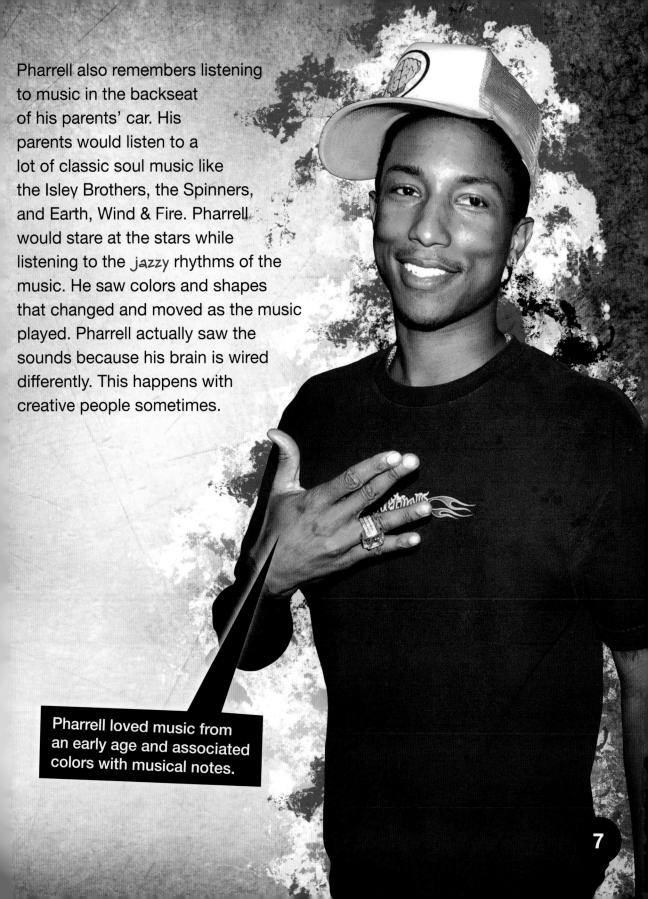

Pharrell also remembers listening to music in the backseat of his parents' car. His parents would listen to a lot of classic soul music like the Isley Brothers, the Spinners, and Earth, Wind & Fire. Pharrell would stare at the stars while listening to the jazzy rhythms of the music. He saw colors and shapes that changed and moved as the music played. Pharrell actually saw the sounds because his brain is wired differently. This happens with creative people sometimes.

Pharrell loved music from an early age and associated colors with musical notes.

Pharrell was not allowed to go outside and play while his parents were at work. So school was the time when he could have fun with his friends. Pharrell wanted to talk about his favorite music and TV shows with his friends during class. He was not a great student, scoring Cs and Ds on his report cards. He would daydream about music instead of paying attention in class.

Pharrell's grandmother was the first to spot his musical ability. Pharrell would take all the pots out of the cabinets and bang on them like drums. His grandmother suggested that he take music classes and play on a real drum set. He had several music teachers and attended a music program for gifted and talented children. There, Pharrell played drums in the band.

In music class, Pharrell learned to read and write music. In an interview years later, Pharrell thanked his band teachers. If they had not seen his talent, Pharrell would not be the star he is today.

Pharrell was in love with hip-hop. When he went home, he listened to artists like Public Enemy and Pete Rock. But the song that changed his life was "Bonita Applebum" by A Tribe Called Quest. That song blew Pharrell's mind.

"Bonita Applebum" was different from other songs. Most songs have a pattern of *verses* and a repeating chorus that is connected by a bridge. The rap group had used a *sample* and looped it. It made the whole song sound like a *bridge*. This created the strange effect Pharrell was hearing. Even as a young man, Pharrell found the technical side of music production fascinating.

Pharrell and Timbaland met in school. Both went on to become famous music producers.

Pharrell did not grow up in the inner city like many popular rappers. He grew up in a *diverse* community. In Virginia Beach, Pharrell was exposed to a wide range of music like hip-hop, punk, and classic rock. He did some break dancing to the old-school music of Afrika Bambaataa and Run-D.M.C. But Pharrell also listened to classic punk bands like the Misfits. And his nickname was "Skateboard P. Pharrell." He never quite fit into one group.

The Neptunes Get Their Feet Wet

Pharrell's summers in Virginia Beach were spent skateboarding on the boardwalk and swimming in the Atlantic Ocean. He has always felt connected to water.

In his hometown, a large statue of Neptune, the Roman god of the sea, overlooks the beach boardwalk. Every year, the Neptune Festival marks the end of summer. Since he was also into space exploration and the planets, Pharrell knew the perfect name for his next band would be the Neptunes.

Pharrell and Chad started playing talent shows around Virginia Beach. It was a good place to be seen because Teddy Riley had just built his studio there. Riley was the famous producer who made new jack swing popular. He had worked with artists like Michael Jackson, Doug E. Fresh, and Bobby Brown. He was a big deal, and Pharrell never expected to get a chance to impress the well-known music producer.

Teddy Riley sent a scout to a talent show where the Neptunes were playing. He immediately signed Pharrell and Chad to his label. The two friends had just graduated from high school, and they had already scored a record deal! It was incredible.

Chad (left) and Pharrell formed the core of the Neptunes. Shae (middle) helped out sometimes.

A few months later, in 1992, Pharrell wrote some of the lyrics for the song "Rump Shaker." It was recorded by Wreckx-n-Effect, a rap group from the early '90s. Pharrell wrote a full verse on the song. The video was very popular but also controversial. In the video, women in bikinis were dancing on the beach. Some said the video was too sexy. But it was popular because it had a funky beat, catchy lyrics, and pretty dancing girls. The album sold more than two million copies. That gave Pharrell his first taste of success.

Pharrell worked with Nicki Minaj and Busta Rhymes on a song called "Twerk It."

Over the next few years, the Neptunes learned a lot from Teddy Riley. He was their mentor, and he taught them about the music business. The Neptunes worked on hits for R&B groups like Blackstreet, SWV, and Total. At this time, Pharrell and Chad were behind the scenes. They were writing and producing. The Neptunes were slowly building a reputation in the industry.

One day, Teddy Riley asked Pharrell to perform a verse on SWV's popular remix for "Right Here." The song used a jazzed-up sample of Michael Jackson's "Human Nature." Pharrell's verse wasn't very good. Teddy Riley cut most of it. He used only one small portion of Pharrell's part. Pharrell only says "S, W, V" at the beginning of the song. But even this small part got him noticed.

During his time with Teddy Riley, Pharrell learned that collaboration is the key to success. He has said that working with others keeps him fresh. Collaboration is what helps him learn and grow. He is also a perfectionist. He says he'll work on a song until it is just right.

Pharrell never works with just one artist at a time. He may be producing an R&B album with Jennifer Hudson while at the same time he's working with the rapper 2 Chainz. Pharrell has said that he's like a sponge. He absorbs the energy in the room and translates it into music.

Here's how Pharrell's mind works. He may be influenced by a smell in the room, what an artist is drinking, or how someone talks. When Pharrell was working with Busta Rhymes and Nicki Minaj on the song "Twerk It," he used the sound of boiling water for the beat. Pharrell creates a personal sound for each artist by finding unique sources of inspiration.

The Neptunes's first major hit as producers was "Superthug" by Noreaga. The song was released in 1998 as the second single from Noreaga's debut album *N.O.R.E.* In addition to producing the record, Pharrell sang the bridge (his favorite part). Kelis, who was a little-known singer at the time, sang the hook.

"Superthug" had a new sound. Chad said that the Neptunes wanted to mix the sounds of hip-hop and rock. The sound of rock and roll depends on the guitar. And that was a problem. Neither Pharrell nor Chad could play the guitar. Instead, they used a clavichord to imitate the sound of a guitar. A clavichord makes a sound that is similar to a guitar, but it has a keyboard. The idea worked. People loved the new sound.

The next year, the Neptunes had the chance to produce their first full album. Kelis was slowly gaining recognition. The Neptunes wanted to give each song on Kelis's album a different color and emotion. They named the album *Kaleidoscope* to reflect the wide range of shades and moods in the songs. *Kaleidoscope* was more popular in Europe than in the United States. But it put Kelis on the map.

"Got Your Money," a track on another album produced by the Neptunes, caught the attention of the music world. The album was by a rapper from the Wu-Tang Clan. "Got Your Money" was the jam of the year.

Pharrell and Chad were still trying to figure out how to make their hip-hop sound stand out. They played around with sampling, beat machines, and live instruments. They were having fun experimenting with hip-hop trends. But soon they would start making trends of their own.

Pharrell and Chad produced their first full album for Kelis.

Songs for the New Millennium

The Neptunes were the new source of hot beats in all the biggest hip-hop and pop songs. Pharrell was on his way to perfecting his sound. It was minimal and futuristic. It helped move hip-hop away from gangsta rap toward danceable club hits.

Pharrell remembered when he first realized that he had made it. It was when he was driving in New York City late one night. He was listening to Funkmaster Flex on the radio. The DJ was playing Mystikal's "Shake It Fast" over and over again. Pharrell couldn't believe it. His voice was echoing all around the big city streets!

Pharrell had ended up singing on Mystikal's hit song by accident. While they were recording, Pharrell suggested that they find a singer who sounded like Curtis Mayfield. Mayfield was a soul singer with a rare voice. Pharrell sang an example to show what the singer should sound like. He used a high falsetto voice. Mystikal loved Pharrell's voice and decided to use it on the track. The rest is history! This falsetto became Pharrell's signature sound.

Right after his success with Mystikal, Pharrell got a call from Jay Z. The famous rapper wanted to work with Pharrell. The Neptunes flew to New York. They created the beat for "I Just Wanna Love U (Give It 2 Me)." Pharrell sang the chorus, and the song was a major success.

The video had celebrity cameos by rappers like Lil' Kim, Jermaine Dupri, and Memphis Bleek. After working with Jay Z, everyone knew about Pharrell and the Neptunes.

Another hit, "Southern Hospitality," by Ludacris, followed. The Atlanta rapper flowed his rhymes over the Neptunes's beat. A long line of performers wanted a chance to collaborate with Pharrell and Chad.

A long list of famous musicians wanted to work with Pharrell.

Pharrell knew that he was more than just a hip-hop producer. He had a passion for all types of music like classical, pop, and especially rock. In 2001, Pharrell broke out of the hip-hop box.

Pharrell wanted to work with Janet Jackson. Jackson is a megastar, and many people write songs for her. She didn't choose to record Pharrell's song, "I'm a Slave 4 U." So he gave the song to Britney Spears.

People warned Pharrell not to work with Spears. They said that working with a pop artist would hurt his career and ruin his reputation. Pharrell refused to listen to the naysayers. "I'm a Slave 4 U" was a smash hit. With the help of Pharrell's funky sound, Britney went from girl singer to grown siren. Her album debuted at number one.

Pharrell was in demand. The next year, Pharrell and the Neptunes wrote Nelly's mega-hit "Hot in Herre." It was Nelly's first number one hit. The Neptunes produced for singers like Mary J. Blige and Usher. And they finally got to work with Janet Jackson. The Neptunes also collaborated with rappers like T.I., Diddy, Ice Cube, and Foxy Brown. They even worked with rock bands like Limp Bizkit and Garbage.

Pharrell worked hard to perfect his signature sound. People were starting to recognize the Neptunes's beats. Pharrell's music was full of digital sounds that seemed to come from video games. Pharrell used blips, beeps, clicks, and whistles. The Neptunes's unique take on hip-hop beats reflected the world's transition to the digital age. They made music for the 21st century.

With his futuristic sound, Pharrell brought his love of space to his music. Pharrell had been interested in outer space since he was a child. He even became friends with astronauts Leland Melvin and Buzz Aldrin. Aldrin was one of the first men to walk on the moon!

Pharrell often flashes the Vulcan greeting. The hand gesture was made famous by the half-alien/half-human character Mr. Spock of the television show and movie series *Star Trek*. When Spock made the sign, he would say, "Live long and prosper." It was similar to and yet very different from the gang signs made by other famous rappers!

Pharrell started Star Trak Entertainment with Chad (his Neptunes partner and longtime friend). He discovered Clipse, a rap duo from Virginia, and signed them to Star Trak. They worked together for some time. And then in 2001, they recorded the song "Grindin'." Pharrell promised that the people were going to feel something they had never felt before. He was right. Pharrell's production was simple and hard-hitting. "Grindin' " became a hip-hop classic. What was different about "Grindin' " is that it didn't rely on sampling.

Hip-hop artists had always used samples. Beats and melodies of older songs, usually soul songs, were remixed to create new songs. But the old song was often recognizable. Pharrell and Chad work differently. They listen to old records to find melodies they like. Then, Chad plays a version of the old song on a keyboard. Pharrell adds drum patterns, changes the keys, and tweaks the song until it is completely new. They use the sample only for inspiration.

Pharrell paved the way for musicians like Kanye West, who use similar techniques. This was an important change for hip-hop. Artists, such as Sean Combs and Dr. Dre, were getting sued in court for sampling music that belonged to other people. Creating new music meant freedom.

Instead of flashing gang signs, Pharrell flashed a sci-fi sign.

Many artists wanted to work with the Neptunes. But Pharrell was determined to work with his idol, Michael Jackson. In 2002, Pharrell and Chad spent all of their energy creating a new album for the King of Pop. Unfortunately, Michael Jackson rejected the songs. Pharrell and Chad were disappointed, but they looked for new opportunities.

Pharrell altered the songs for Justin Timberlake's first solo album. The star was looking to break away from his hit boy band, 'N Sync. He wanted a more mature sound. Pharrell brought Timberlake to his recording studio in Virginia Beach. For six weeks, Pharrell became Timberlake's mentor. Pharrell urged the young singer to show all sides of his personality.

Pharrell knew that Justin loved soul music. They both shared a love for Earth, Wind & Fire. Pharrell used this as inspiration. He brought funk, soul, and classic R&B to Timberlake's first solo album. *Justified* was a huge success. People compared Justin Timberlake to Michael Jackson. Pharrell had helped bring out Justin's talent. *Justified* sold millions of copies around the world. Justin was a megastar, and Pharrell continued to grow his reputation as a mega-producer. Later, Michael Jackson expressed regret for not using Pharrell's songs.

In 2002, Pharrell had five top singles on the Billboard charts. The Neptunes worked with almost every popular artist at that time, like Snoop Dogg, Toni Braxton, Royce da 5'9", Nelly, Common, LL Cool J, Usher, Ja Rule, Jay Z, and Busta Rhymes.

At one point, Pharrell had worked on nearly half of all the new music that was playing on the radio. He dominated the airwaves and created the trends within popular music. Pharrell was a musical powerhouse.

The Neptunes had created an album for Michael Jackson. When he turned it down, they worked with Justin Timberlake instead.

In 2003, the Neptunes released *Clones*. The album was a compilation album of their top rap collaborations. The album had hits by Clipse, Ludacris, Snoop Dogg, Busta Rhymes, and Nelly. They put the album out on their new label, Star Trak Entertainment. That same year, Star Trak also released Kelis's album *Tasty*. The single "Milkshake" was a huge hit.

In 2003, Pharrell experienced another first. He was interviewed by one of his idols, Michael Jackson. Even though the King of Pop had rejected his songs two years earlier, Pharrell was excited to talk to the legend. Pharrell and Michael Jackson talked about what inspired them and their love of classic soul groups like Sly & the Family Stone and the Isley Brothers. They discussed the good and bad parts of being superstars. They discussed the changes they had brought to the music world, and how it felt to be targeted in the media.

Years later, Pharrell finally did get to work on a Michael Jackson song. The experience was bittersweet. Michael Jackson passed away on June 25, 2009. A few weeks after that, Pharrell recorded a remix of the Jackson 5's "Never Can Say Goodbye." Although he did not get a chance to collaborate with the King of Pop in the studio, Pharrell laid his signature sound behind Michael Jackson's voice.

In 2004, Pharrell and Star Trak made a deal with Snoop Dogg's Doggystyle Records. Pharrell and Snoop released "Drop It Like It's Hot." It was the smash hit of that summer. The song was especially noticeable for its minimalist production. Only a drum machine, a few keyboards, and mouth sounds make up the beat. It was classic Pharrell, and people loved it.

Pharrell received two Grammy Awards in 2004. One was for Producer of the Year with the Neptunes. The other was for Best Pop Vocal Album for his work on Justin Timberlake's *Justified*

Pharrell and Timberlake both won Grammy Awards for their work on *Justified*.

Where Rock Meets Hip-Hop

While the Neptunes were making it big as producers, Pharrell and Chad had an ongoing side project with their high school friend Shae Haley. Back in 2001, they formed the group N.E.R.D., which stands for "No-one Ever Really Dies." The idea comes from a basic belief that energy cannot be created or destroyed; it can only change forms.

N.E.R.D. also spells "nerd." Being nerdy is the exact opposite of the street-tough image that most rappers project. It is also very different from the *suave* image that Diddy is famous for. But it reflects the interests of Pharrell and his friends. They care about science and art. They are not afraid to be different.

In Search Of... was N.E.R.D.'s first album. The original version of the album was released in 2001 with all digital sounds. No live instruments were played. N.E.R.D. used beat machines and mixers to make their music. But the band decided it sounded too much like the Neptunes, so they re-recorded the album in 2002. This time they hired the rock group Spymob to add live instruments to the music.

N.E.R.D. worked with cutting-edge visual artists on the album. Shepard Fairey created the album's logo. Today, Fairey is famous for the Barack Obama "Hope" poster. Pharrell also did a photo shoot with Terry Richardson for the album's cover. Today, Richardson is a successful fashion photographer.

N.E.R.D. played their first show with the Beastie Boys. Pharrell's band learned a lot about performing for a crowd from the more experienced trio. Pharrell also learned by watching videos of punk bands he listened to in high school like the Dead Kennedys and Suicidal Tendencies. They mixed the high energy of punk shows with hip-hop sounds to create a new concert experience.

With his band N.E.R.D., Pharrell was no longer behind the scenes. He was right out on stage!

In 2004, Pharrell released *Fly or Die*, his second album with N.E.R.D. Instead of hiring a band as with their first album, the group learned to play all of the instruments. Pharrell played drums and guitar, and contributed vocals on the album.

Fly or Die was ahead of its time. N.E.R.D. offered special items to fans. A limited edition was released with Nike's Dunk High shoe designed by Pharrell. Fans could also purchase N.E.R.D. action figures or a special N.E.R.D. T-shirt.

In 2008, N.E.R.D. released their third album, *Seeing Sounds*. The title came from Pharrell's youth when he was hearing music in color in the backseat of his parents' car. Since that time, Pharrell had learned that this was caused by a condition known as synesthesia.

Some of the most successful artists and musicians in history have had synesthesia. People like Duke Ellington and Stevie Wonder both saw colors when listening to music. Even Pharrell's good friend, the rapper and producer Kanye West, has the condition.

In 2010, N.E.R.D. released their fourth album titled *Nothing*. Pharrell said they were taking their sound in a new direction. He believed that the world was entering a new phase, one that is both a little exciting and a little scary. Pharrell loves the creative side of new technology like the iPad. But he is also aware of the dark side of technology, such as environmental disasters like the Gulf Coast oil spill. Pharrell wants to help people face the future with hope.

N.E.R.D.'s albums have never sold as well as the hits Pharrell has written and produced for other people. Even so, the band has loyal followers around the world.

For the album *Fly or Die*, Pharrell returned to drumming. He also sang and played guitar.

Pharrell Rising

Pharrell explored his passions through N.E.R.D. And he experienced major success as a music producer. He started a label and helped develop talent. He worked to give artists a signature sound. In addition to Clipse, he signed the rapper Slim Thug and released his debut, *Already Platinum*. The album debuted at number two on the Billboard music charts. His group projects with the Neptunes, N.E.R.D., and Star Trak made him very successful. But Pharrell was ready to soar on his own.

In 2006, Pharrell released his debut album as a solo artist, called *In My Mind*. Artists like Gwen Stefani, Kanye West, and Jay Z made guest appearances. The album sold really well in the United Kingdom. International fans loved him.

The album was remade into *Out of My Mind* with instrumentals from Questlove and James Poyser from the Roots. Although the remix album was never officially released, *Out of My Mind* is a cult classic for serious Pharrell fans.

In interviews, Pharrell talks about his disappointment with his first solo album. He believed that he had to talk about money, girls, and cars in order to be successful like other rappers. But he wasn't being true to himself. He called *In My Mind* an album "without purpose."

Critics and fans in the United States were *lukewarm* about Pharrell's debut as a solo artist. Pharrell loved music, but he was getting frustrated with the industry. He was bored with EDM (electronic dance music). It seemed that was all people wanted to hear. Pharrell was feeling boxed in by the style he had created. He needed a break and some inspiration. So Pharrell turned from sound to sight. He got into art.

Pharrell and Gwen Stefani worked together on her big hit "Hollaback Girl," and she appeared on his solo album *In My Mind*.

Pharrell found a new passion in fashion!

Pharrell slowed down his music production to focus on fashion. He wasn't interested in competing with Sean John by Diddy or Roca Wear by Jay Z. Pharrell wanted to make clothes that were like art.

In 2003, Pharrell teamed up with Nigo, the Japanese fashion icon. Nigo had made his name in the Japanese fashion industry with the clothing line Bathing Ape (or BAPE for short). BAPE is a very popular street-wear brand.

Nigo and Pharrell met while Pharrell was working in Tokyo. Pharrell was recording a song for a video game. Nigo was a huge fan of Pharrell's work. He knew that Pharrell was into fashion, but he didn't know that Pharrell was already planning his fashion line.

Reebok had wanted to work with Pharrell on a line of sneakers that would compete with Jay Z's S. Carter collection and 50 Cent's G-Unit line. But Pharrell wanted to make more than collectible sneakers. He also wanted to make clothing and accessories. In the end, the relationship with Reebok didn't work out.

Pharrell said that working with Nigo "made his dream reality." Pharrell and Nigo launched two brands called Billionaire Boys Club (BBC) and Icecream. Pharrell's clothing is most popular in Asia. He has stores in Tokyo, Hong Kong, London, and New York.

Nigo introduced Pharrell to Japanese culture. Pharrell calls Japan a second home. Mixing cultures and styles, Pharrell brought a new fashion sense to hip-hop. And he found a new passion.

Pharrell was on his way to becoming a fashion icon. In 2005, he was voted the best-dressed man in the world by *Esquire* magazine. A few years later, Marc Jacobs, the lead designer for the famous fashion label Louis Vuitton, asked Pharrell and Nigo to bring their signature style to the brand. They created the Millionaire line of sunglasses. They were so successful that Pharrell branched out. He also designed very expensive gold jewelry for Louis Vuitton.

In 2009, Pharrell moved into the world of fine art. He collaborated with the sculptor Takashi Murakami and Jacob Arabo (Jacob the Jeweler) on a sculpture called *The Simple Things*. Pharrell wanted to show how oftentimes the simple pleasures in life are overlooked.

Pharrell chose seven items, including a bottle of Johnson's baby lotion, a bag of Doritos, and a can of Pepsi. Those items were covered with over 26,000 precious gems. Pharrell said he wanted to symbolize how people value things in their lives. To Pharrell, small things like the taste of Pepsi or the smell of baby lotion are what makes him happy. *The Simple Things* sold for more than $2 million in less than 30 minutes.

In 2010, Pharrell created a line of men's clothing for Moncler, a European company. He worked with Bionic Yarn, a state-of-the-art fabric company. The fabric was made from recycled plastic bottles. He also designed a fashionable bulletproof vest. Pharrell was using fashion to make a political statement. He showed that instead of using energy for violence, you could use it to help make the world better.

In 2014, Pharrell debuted the collection Raw for the Oceans. It is a line of denim clothing made from plastic taken from the world's oceans.

Pharrell designed sunglasses and jewelry as well as clothes.

Pharrell and Helen Lasichanh had a son in 2008 they named Rocket Ayer.

Pharrell created the documentary *Tokyo Rising* to support Japan, his second home. In the film, he interviewed young Japanese artists who were thinking about the future of their country after the 3/11 tragedy.

On March 11, 2011, an earthquake and tsunami hit Japan with a one-two punch. Over a million buildings were damaged or destroyed. More than 20,000 people were killed or injured.

Tokyo Rising shows how the young people of Japan remember the 3/11 tragedy, but also how they are moving forward. They are using new business models and online resources like Twitter to rebuild, and they look to the future with hope.

In 2012, Pharrell continued to explore new forms. He published a book called *Pharrell: Places and Spaces I've Been*. Instead of highlighting his own story, Pharrell features the words and art of his collaborators. He calls it a retrospective of people who have helped his wildest dreams come true. Never again would Pharrell make anything "without purpose."

In Pharrell's book, Jay Z recalls what he discussed with his friend the Notorious B.I.G. on the night Biggie was killed. Kanye West shares how he and Pharrell bonded over synesthesia. Buzz Aldrin speaks with Pharrell about space exploration and the possibility of traveling to Mars. Anna Wintour, the editor-in-chief of *Vogue* magazine, contributed to his essay on fashion.

Back in 2008, Pharrell had his most important collaboration of all. He had a son, Rocket Ayer Williams, with Helen Lasichanh, a model and fashion designer. Pharrell once said that Rocket was "the best song I've ever co-created." Pharrell and Helen married in a small, private ceremony in 2013. A private person, Pharrell left this collaboration out of his book!

Live Long and Prosper

In 2010, Pharrell began another important relationship. He worked with Hans Zimmer, the famous film *composer*, on the animated film *Despicable Me*. Together they composed and produced the music for that movie. Pharrell had the chance to work with a full orchestra and many guest stars.

Pharrell said that animation is fun and challenging. Creating a film *score* is very different from creating a pop album. For a movie, the composer has to follow the suggestions from the director. The music has to match the emotion and mood of a scene. If the scene in the movie was supposed to make you cry, then Pharrell had to match that sadness.

Pharrell returned to work on *Despicable Me 2* in 2012. He had trouble matching the music to one particular scene. Pharrell tried about nine times before he got it right. *Ultimately*, his dedication paid off. The song "Happy" was the result.

Pharrell released the first ever 24-hour music video for "Happy." In it, 400 dancers from every walk of life dance in any way that made them happy. The dance party lasts for a full day! Many guest stars, like Odd Future, Magic Johnson, and Janaelle Monae, helped make the video a smash.

By August 2014, the video had been viewed nearly 400 million times on YouTube! People all over the world uploaded their own music videos for "Happy." They shared their own expressions of happiness.

Pharrell and Zimmer made a great team. They worked together again on the 84th Academy Awards in 2012. That job involved scoring over 100 musical cues for the live show. In 2014, they also co-composed the score for *The Amazing Spider Man II*.

Pharrell wrote the hit song "Happy" while he was working on *Despicable Me 2* with Hans Zimmer.

Pharrell worked with Robin Thicke on one of the biggest hits of 2013, "Blurred Lines."

42

Pharrell wanted to work with Lauryn Hill. She was a legend in the hip-hop world for her rap style and beautiful singing voice. But she had disappeared from the music scene. If anyone could convince her to come back, it would be Pharrell. After all, in 2009 the Neptunes had won Producer of the Decade.

One day, Pharrell had the chance to talk with Hill. She said she didn't want the same music he made for everyone else. She wanted the "other." Pharrell was blown away. Although the project didn't work out, Hill's words stuck in Pharrell's head.

He also noticed young people on the Internet who were unique and creative. Pharrell wanted to make a space where people from all backgrounds and cultures could come together. Pharrell's *i am OTHER* movement is a space for freedom of creativity.

On his website, Pharrell says, "*i am OTHER* celebrates people who push society forward. The thinkers. The innovators. The outcasts. History has proven that it's the rule breakers who have the power to change the world."

Pharrell had moved far from his musical beginnings into art, fashion, films, and books. He had even started movements! But he never gave up music. And his biggest hits were yet to come.

Pharrell's work with the electronic duo Daft Punk was a huge success. Pharrell found himself back in the spotlight with "Get Lucky," and "Lose Yourself to Dance." The music was lively and soulful. It made people want to dance. "Get Lucky" was number one on the charts. A few weeks later, Pharrell released the song "Blurred Lines" with singer Robin Thicke. Pharrell was all over the radio. It was 2013, and he was leading the industry with passion and joy.

Pharrell released his second solo album *G I R L* in March of 2014. Pharrell said he dedicated *G I R L* to women. He said that without the support of women in his life, he'd be nothing. The album features guest appearances by female artists, including Kelly Osbourne, Alicia Keys, and Miley Cyrus.

Pharrell also teamed up with some longtime friends like Timbaland, Hans Zimmer, Justin Timberlake, and Daft Punk. *G I R L* had the spirit of collaboration that Pharrell has embraced throughout his long career. With the help of the song "Happy," *G I R L* was Pharrell's best-selling solo album to date. The year got even better. Pharrell won a second Grammy for Producer of the Year.

What does the future hold for Pharrell? He would like to create animated cartoons that show his unique style. He says he'd like to be the first international music producer. He imagines finding musical collaborators in places like Africa, Germany, Japan, and Taiwan.

Someone once asked Pharrell what inspires him. He said, "That which does not exist." In other words, Pharrell is always looking for a way to do what has not yet been done.

Pharrell is willing to take risks in order to stay true to himself. You could say that he drums to his own beat and keeps us happy. His willingness to be "other" has made him more successful than he could have ever dreamed. The only dream he has not yet lived is being an astronaut and exploring space. But maybe he will get there yet!

Pharrell keeps pushing himself to do something that hasn't been done before.

Vocabulary

accessories	(noun)	items that are worn in addition to clothes, such as belts, sunglasses, shoes, pocketbooks, etc.
airwaves	(noun)	the sound put out by radio stations
Billboard	(noun)	a music magazine and website
bittersweet	(adjective)	happy and sad at the same time
bridge	(noun)	the part of a song that connects the verse to the chorus
cameo	(noun)	a brief appearance by a celebrity
collaboration	(noun)	two or more people working on the same project
compilation	(noun)	a collection
composer	(noun)	a person who writes music
controversial	(adjective)	likely to start public disagreement
cutting-edge	(adjective)	new and different
debut	(adjective)	first
diverse	(adjective)	coming from many different backgrounds
documentary	(noun)	a nonfiction movie
falsetto	(adjective)	singing that is much higher than your normal voice
hook	(noun)	a catchy tune or beat that helps makes a song easy to remember
icon	(noun)	a famous person
innovative	(adjective)	inventive
instrumental	(noun)	music without words
jazzy	(adjective)	fun and lively
limited edition	(noun)	something produced in small numbers
lukewarm	(adjective)	not good but not terrible
mentor	(noun)	someone who acts as a guide or a teacher
minimal	(adjective)	very clean and simple
naysayer	(noun)	people who criticize and doubt you

new jack swing	(noun)	a style of hip-hop that mixed rapping and singing
outcast	(noun)	a person who doesn't fit in with the crowd
perfectionist	(noun)	someone who won't stop working until something is perfect in every way
powerhouse	(noun)	someone who is important in his or her profession
producer	(noun)	the person who helps a musical artist create songs and a distinctive sound
prosper	(verb)	to live well
R&B	(noun)	a style of soulful singing
regret	(noun)	sorrow
remix	(noun)	a new version of a song
retrospective	(noun)	a collection of past work
sample	(noun)	a small piece of music from other songs
score	(noun)	the music that is written for a movie or play
scout	(noun)	someone who looks for new talent
sculptor	(noun)	an artist that makes 3-D art
signature	(adjective)	something that is associated with a particular person
siren	(noun)	a sexy singer
street-wear	(noun)	casual-style clothes
suave	(adjective)	elegant and well dressed
symbolize	(verb)	to show something without saying it directly
synesthesia	(noun)	a condition that causes people to experience overlapping senses
trio	(noun)	a group of three
ultimately	(adverb)	finally
verse	(noun)	the parts of a song that comes between the repeating chorus

Photo Credits